P9-DCV-274

A Special Gift

_____

Presented to:

_____

From:

_____

Date:

A Lasting Heritage for Your Children

A Father's Legacy

Your Life Story in Your Own Words

Copyright © 2001 by J. Countryman, a division of
Thomas Nelson, Inc., Nashville, Tennessee 37214

Project editor—Terri Gibbs

A J. Countryman Book

*Designed by Koechel Peterson Design, Inc.,
Minneapolis, Minnesota*

ISBN: 0-8499-5523-8

Printed and bound in Mexico

Contents

Introduction

. . . .

"What grade did you get in high school English, Dad?" "What did you do on your first date?" Sound familiar?

Your son or daughter has probably asked these questions and many more. Why? Curiosity partly, but mostly because they care—about you. They want to know what you did when you were growing up because they want to know you.

That is the purpose of this book, which is a book about you—your family history, your childhood memories, humorous incidents, and meaningful traditions from your life. It is a personal biography just waiting to be written. Yes, there are planes to catch, meetings to attend, grass to mow, and the car to wash, but those are not a legacy you can pass on to your child. This book is.

Presented in a twelve-month format, this journal provides an array of questions your son or daughter might ask with space for your answers. Questions like,

"Describe the most fun you ever had on a Fourth of July." Or "When you went to a ball game as a boy, what kind of food did you eat?" Or "What is the nicest thing you ever did for your mother and father?"

These questions will help you write down the special memories, thoughts, and ideas you want to share with your children. You may choose to complete the journal in a few days, a few weeks, or throughout the course of the year. When you have filled in all of the pages you will have a loving memoir—a spiritual legacy—to pass on to your children. They will cherish this book about you for a lifetime.

This book is for fathers of all ages, because it is never too early or too late to share your life with those you love. May *A Father's Legacy* draw you closer to your children as you share this memoir of your life . . . straight from your heart to theirs

Personal Portrait

....

your full given name ————————————————————————————.

your date of birth ————————————————————————————.

your place of birth————————————————————————————.

your mother's full name ————————————————————————.

   the place and date of her birth————————————————————.

your father's full name ————————————————————————.

   the place and date of his birth————————————————————.

the names of your paternal grandparents ——————————————.

   the places and dates of their births ——————————————————.

the names of your maternal grandparents——————————————.

   the places and dates of their births ——————————————————.

the names of your siblings ————————————————————.

   the places and dates of their births ——————————————————.

————————————————————————————.

————————————————————————————.

————————————————————————————.

the date and place of your marriage _____ .

the full given name of your wife _____ .

the names and birth dates of your children _____

_____

_____

What is your favorite?

sport _____ .   Bible verse _____

book _____ .   hymn or song _____

leisure activity _____ .   vacation spot _____ .

dessert _____ .   type of food _____

author _____ .   sports team _____ .

January

Our stories are
inextricably interwoven.
What you do is part of my story;
what I do is part of yours.

DANIEL TAYLOR

—January—

Who gave you your name and why?
Did you have a nickname? How did you get it?

_____
_____
_____
_____
_____
_____
_____
_____
_____
_____
_____
_____
_____
_____

Describe your childhood home.
What was your favorite room?

*W*ere you baptized or dedicated as an infant?
If so, where and by whom?_____

_____

_____

_____

_____

*D*id you attend church as a young boy?
What are your earliest memories of church?_____

_____

_____

_____

_____

_____

_____

—January—

Where did your father go to work every day
and what did he do? Did his work interest you?_____

_____
_____
_____

Did your mother have a job
or did she work at home?_____

_____
_____
_____
_____
_____
_____

What was your favorite sport or outdoor activity? Why was this your favorite?

*D*escribe your grandparents.
What did you enjoy most about them?

_____

_____

_____

_____

_____

_____

_____

_____

_____

_____

_____

_____

_____

_____

Recall for me five
of the most important lessons
you have learned in life.

_____

_____

_____

_____

_____

_____

_____

_____

_____

_____

February

Gratitude is the

memory of the heart.

—◆—

MASSIEU

How far did you have to travel to attend elementary, junior high, and high school, and how did you get there? _____

_____

_____

_____

_____

_____

_____

_____

_____

_____

_____

_____

*Who gave you your first Bible
and how old where you when you received it.
How did it influence your life?*_____

_____

_____

_____

_____

_____

_____

_____

_____

_____

_____

When did you become a Christian?
How did your life change? _____

_____

_____

_____

_____

_____

_____

_____

_____

_____

_____

_____

_____

_____

*W*hen you were growing up, did you
have any animals? What were their names?
Was it important to you to have a pet? _____

_____

_____

_____

_____

_____

_____

_____

_____

_____

_____

_____

—February—

What chores did you have to
do when you were growing up?
Did you get an allowance? How much was it?

_____
_____
_____
_____
_____
_____
_____
_____
_____
_____
_____

—February—

*W*ho gave you your first job?
What kind of job was it?
*How much money did you make?*_____

_____

_____

_____

_____

_____

_____

_____

_____

_____

_____

_____

Share your idea of
what makes a good friend.

_____

_____

_____

_____

_____

_____

_____

_____

_____

_____

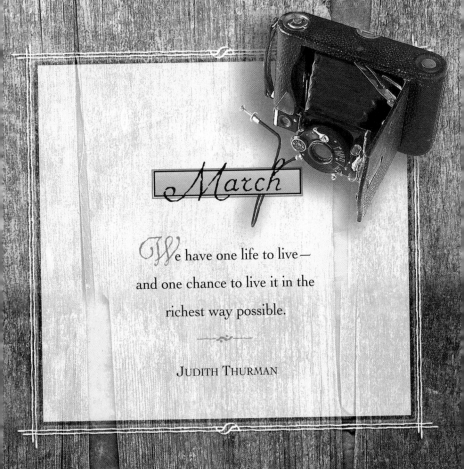

March

We have one life to live—
and one chance to live it in the
richest way possible.

JUDITH THURMAN

—January—

*Did you pray as a young boy?
If so, can you remember a specific prayer?
Who taught you to pray?* _____

_____

_____

_____

_____

_____

_____

_____

_____

_____

_____

_____

*D*id you have a television when you were growing up?
What was your favorite program? Why? _____

_____

_____

_____

_____

*D*escribe your favorite
pastime or hobby as a child. _____

_____

_____

_____

_____

_____

*Who was your favorite teacher?
How did that teacher influence your life?*

_____

_____

_____

_____

_____

_____

_____

_____

_____

_____

_____

—March—

Did you ever have a special hideaway or clubhouse? Describe it for me.

31

—March—

*I*n high school, what extracurricular
activities did you enjoy most?
Why did you choose those activities? _____

_____
_____
_____
_____
_____
_____
_____
_____
_____
_____
_____

—*March*—

What is the nicest thing you ever did for your mother and father?

—March—

*D*id you admire a famous person?
What made that person admirable?

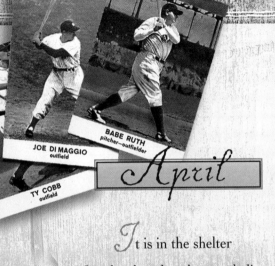

JOE DiMAGGIO
outfield

TY COBB
outfield

BABE RUTH
pitcher–outfielder

April

*I*t is in the shelter

of each other that the people live.

IRISH PROVERB

During childhood, who was your best friend?
Share some of your fondest memories of fun times together.

_____

_____

_____

_____

_____

_____

_____

_____

_____

_____

_____

_____

*Was there a special person
who helped you in your Christian walk?
Share something about that person.*

*As a teenager did you rebel or do things
your parents wouldn't have approved of?
How do you feel about that now?*_____

_____

_____

_____

_____

_____

_____

_____

_____

_____

_____

_____

When did you have your first date?
Tell me about it.

What is your favorite memory of your mother?
Why is it so special to you? _____

_____

_____

_____

_____

_____

_____

_____

_____

_____

_____

_____

_____

—*April*—

What image of your father is the most striking in your memory? Why that image?

_____

_____

_____

_____

_____

_____

_____

_____

_____

_____

_____

*L*ist one special memory
about each of your brothers and sisters.

May

*W*ho, being loved, is poor?

OSCAR WILDE

—May—

If you were to find an old toy box in your attic, what toys would you remember most fondly? Why? _____

_____

_____

_____

_____

_____

_____

_____

_____

_____

_____

_____

*H*ow old were you when you understood
that God loves you? How did that affect your life? _____

_____

_____

_____

_____

_____

_____

_____

_____

_____

_____

_____

*W*hat were your family finances like when
you were growing up? How did that affect you?_____

_____

_____

_____

_____

_____

*W*hat kind of car did your family drive?
Were you proud of it or embarrassed by it? Why?

_____

_____

_____

_____

_____

*H*ow often did your family go to church? What pastor or Sunday school teacher do you remember most? How did that person influence you?

_____

_____

_____

_____

_____

_____

_____

_____

_____

_____

_____

Did your family attend family reunions? What activities did everyone enjoy? Tell me about your favorite cousins, aunts, or uncles. _____

_____

_____

_____

_____

_____

_____

_____

_____

_____

_____

_____

_____

—May—

*If you went to college
or to a career training school,
where did you go and why?*

Share some principles from
Scripture on which you have
chosen to build your life.

_____

_____

_____

_____

_____

_____

_____

_____

_____

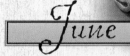

June

$\mathcal{T}$he linking of generations,

the historical lineage of family,

the sharing of love . . .

give purpose to life.

——◦——

GEORGE LANDBERG

If you learned to play a musical instrument, tell me your memories of lessons, practice, and your music teacher. If not, what instrument did you want to play and why?

_____
_____
_____
_____
_____
_____
_____
_____
_____
_____
_____

—June—

*W*hat were your youthful goals and ambitions for life?
Which ones have you been able to fulfill? _____

_____

_____

_____

_____

_____

_____

_____

_____

_____

_____

_____

_____

*H*ow old were you when you
met Mom? What attracted you to her?

_____
_____
_____
_____
_____
_____
_____
_____
_____
_____
_____
_____
_____
_____

*W*hen did you know that Mom was the
"one and only one" for you? How did you know? _____

_____

_____

_____

*S*hare a memory about the
way you proposed to Mom. _____

_____

_____

_____

_____

—June—

Tell me about your wedding day.
What happened? How did you feel?
Were you nervous, scared, happy? _____

_____

_____

_____

_____

_____

_____

_____

_____

_____

_____

—June—

*W*here did you go on your honeymoon?
Describe at least one humorous thing that
happened to you and Mom. _____

_____

_____

_____

_____

_____

_____

_____

_____

_____

_____

*W*hat do you love best
about Mom now? _____

_____

_____

_____

_____

_____

_____

_____

_____

_____

_____

_____

_____

July

Somehow, year after year,

Dad managed to take us on vacations

he couldn't afford to provide, in order

to make memories that we couldn't

afford to be without.

RICHARD EXLEY

—July—

*Describe the most fun you
ever had on a Fourth of July.* _____

_____

_____

_____

_____

_____

_____

_____

_____

_____

_____

_____

Tell me about your family summer outings when you were young. Did you go camping? Fishing? Swimming?

_____

_____

_____

_____

_____

_____

_____

_____

_____

_____

_____

_____

—*July*—

*If you served in the armed forces,
describe how your time in the service affected your life.
If you did not serve, how did this affect your life?*

_____

_____

_____

_____

_____

_____

_____

_____

_____

_____

_____

*W*here do you stand politically? Do you lean toward the left or the right? Who, if anyone, has most greatly influenced your current political views? _____

_____

_____

_____

_____

_____

_____

_____

_____

_____

*D*id a tragedy ever strike your family?
If so, how did it affect you? _____

_____

_____

_____

_____

_____

_____

_____

_____

_____

_____

_____

Did you ever go to summer camp?
Camping with the Boy Scouts?
Share one unforgettable memory. _____

_____

_____

_____

_____

_____

_____

_____

_____

_____

_____

Share a favorite poem,
passage of writing, or some
quotes that have been especially
meaningful in your life.

_____

_____

_____

_____

_____

_____

_____

_____

August

When I come home
from work and see those little noses
pressed against the window pane,
then I know I am a success.

PAUL FAULKNER

Did you enjoy reading as a boy?
What were some of the most memorable books you read?

_____

_____

_____

_____

Is there any one book or author who helped you to
develop a philosophy of life? Share some of those insights.

_____

_____

_____

_____

What is your favorite
way to spend a day of leisure?_____

_____
_____
_____
_____
_____
_____
_____
_____
_____
_____
_____
_____
_____

—August—

What places in the world would you still like to visit? Why?

*H*ow do you enjoy helping people?
Share about a time when you helped someone in need.

—August—

*In what ways are you like
your mother? Like your father?*

_____

_____

_____

_____

_____

_____

_____

_____

_____

_____

_____

_____

*L*ooking back in life, what one thing would you have done differently? Why? _____

_____

_____

_____

_____

_____

_____

_____

_____

_____

_____

_____

_____

How have your ideas about
God changed from when you were young? _____

_____

_____

_____

_____

_____

_____

_____

_____

_____

_____

_____

_____

September

What lies behind
us and what lies before us
are tiny matters compared
to what lies within us.

———◦———

RALPH WALDO EMERSON

Did you learn mechanics or woodworking as a young person? How and when? What were some of your most memorable projects? _____

_____

_____

_____

_____

_____

_____

_____

_____

_____

_____

_____

*T*ell about a special outing you took with your dad. What makes this a poignant memory for you?_____

_____

_____

_____

_____

_____

_____

_____

_____

_____

_____

_____

*A*s a young person did you
volunteer for work in church, community,
or social services? Tell me about it.

_____

_____

_____

_____

_____

_____

_____

_____

_____

_____

_____

*W*hat special talents did your parents nurture
in you? How have you developed those talents?_____

_____

_____

*W*hat would you still like to learn to do?
Why? _____

_____

_____

_____

_____

When did you move away from home?
Describe where you lived and how you felt about it. _____

_____

_____

_____

_____

_____

_____

_____

_____

_____

_____

_____

_____

_____

—September—

*W*hat are
your spiritual strengths? _____

_____

_____

_____

*H*ow would you
like to grow spiritually? _____

_____

_____

_____

_____

_____

How do you describe
"success"?

_____

_____

_____

_____

_____

_____

_____

_____

_____

_____

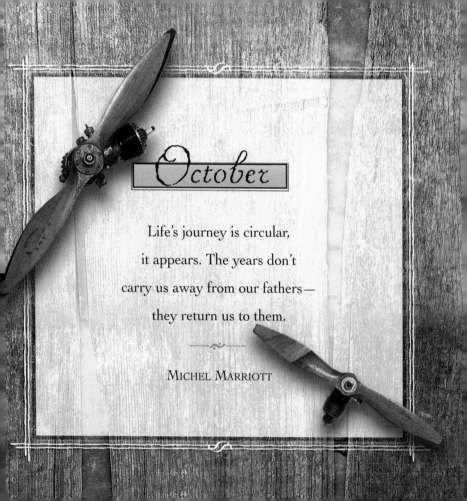

October

Life's journey is circular,
it appears. The years don't
carry us away from our fathers—
they return us to them.

MICHEL MARRIOTT

What did your family like to do on weekends? Describe one particularly memorable one.

_____

_____

_____

_____

_____

_____

_____

_____

_____

_____

_____

_____

Share a hilarious travel experience.

_____

_____

_____

_____

_____

_____

_____

_____

_____

_____

_____

_____

_____

What Bible verse or Scripture puzzles you the most? Which blesses you the most? Why? _____

_____

_____

_____

_____

_____

_____

_____

_____

_____

_____

_____

_____

*What events in life have strengthened your belief in prayer?*_____

_____

_____

_____

_____

_____

_____

_____

_____

_____

_____

_____

_____

—October—

Do you have a favorite sports team? Why is that one your favorite?

What is the most frightening thing that has ever happened to you? How did you handle the experience?

_____

_____

_____

_____

_____

_____

_____

_____

_____

_____

_____

_____

When and where did you buy
your first house or piece of real estate?
Describe the significance this held for you.

_____

_____

_____

_____

_____

_____

_____

_____

_____

_____

_____

_____

_____

November

*G*od calls each
generation to pass down
spiritual truth to the next.

———✦———

DENNIS RAINEY

What is your most treasured possession and why?

_____

_____

_____

_____

_____

_____

_____

_____

_____

_____

_____

_____

_____

—November—

What two people have made the greatest spiritual impact on your life? What made them so significant to you?

_____

_____

_____

_____

_____

_____

_____

_____

_____

_____

_____

_____

*When you were a new father,
what was your greatest fear? Your greatest joy?*_____

_____

_____

_____

_____

_____

_____

_____

_____

_____

_____

_____

_____

*W*hat is your most
vivid memory about my childhood? _____

_____

_____

_____

*W*hat would you change
about my childhood if you could? _____

_____

_____

_____

_____

_____

_____

Describe a fond Thanksgiving memory. What makes this special to you? _____

_____

_____

_____

_____

_____

_____

_____

_____

_____

_____

_____

— November —

What are some things from your childhood that you are thankful for? _____

_____

_____

_____

_____

_____

_____

_____

_____

_____

_____

_____

_____

_____

Tell me what four things
you would never leave behind
on a trip and explain why.

_____

_____

_____

_____

_____

_____

_____

_____

_____

December

$\mathcal{T}$hose who loved you
and were helped by you will
remember you. So carve your name
on hearts and not on marble.

C. H. SPURGEON

*W*hat is the best Christmas present
you ever received? Why was that the best?

_____

_____

_____

_____

_____

_____

_____

_____

_____

_____

_____

_____

_____

*T*ell about a memorable
Christmas visit with relatives. _____

_____
_____
_____
_____
_____
_____
_____
_____
_____
_____
_____
_____

—December—

W

**hat would be the most wonderful
gift you could receive? Why?** _____

_____

_____

_____

_____

_____

_____

_____

_____

_____

_____

_____

*T*ell me about a time when
God answered a specific prayer for you _____

_____

_____

_____

_____

_____

_____

_____

_____

_____

_____

_____

_____

What would you like to see happen in the next ten years in your life? In the world?

As you look back in life, name three of the most fantastic changes that have taken place in the world. How have these affected your life? _____

_____

_____

_____

_____

_____

_____

_____

_____

_____

_____

What hat word best describes your life?
Explain why.

_____

_____

_____

_____

_____

_____

_____

_____

_____

_____

_____

Share some of
your insights for working
well with others.

_____

_____

_____

_____

_____

_____

_____

_____

_____

*Record here your ideas on what
it takes for a husband and wife to maintain a
healthy marriage.*

_____

_____

_____

_____

_____

_____

_____

_____

_____

_____

Share with me your
father's attitude toward life
and how that affected you.

_____

_____

_____

_____

_____

_____

_____

_____

_____

Share some tips

for a great vacation.

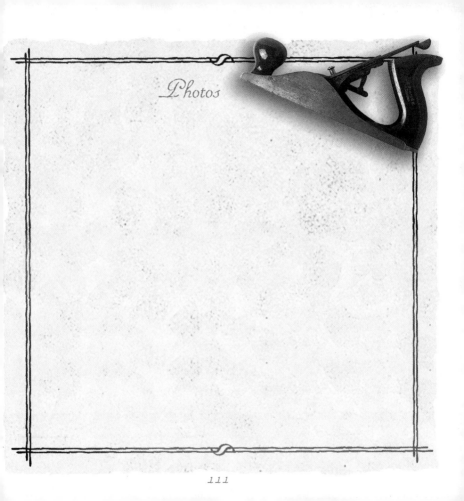

Photos

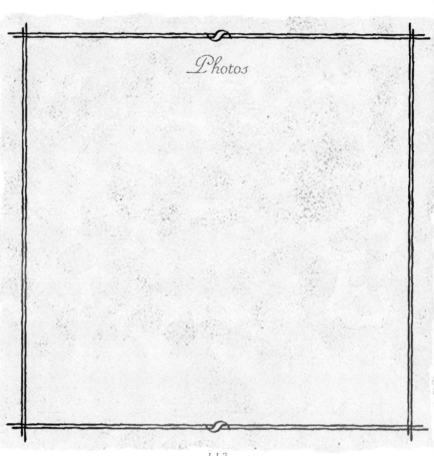

Photos